SINGAPORE HOLIDAY TRAVELOGUE

ART & SCIENCE OF DESIGNING A CLASSY YET POCKET FRIENDLY, SELF EXPLORATORY SG FAMILY VACATION. FOREWORD BY - TAMAL BANDYOPADHYAY

ASHIESH KAPOOR

I dedicate this book to my parents, Smt. & Shri M. Kapur, whose blessings and good wishes have been a constant source of encouragement in my endeavour to pen an off-beat travel book, that combines the art and science of planning for a classy, stylish yet affordable, pocket-friendly Singapore holiday.

ᗢᗢᗢ

A big thank you to my wife for being a perpetual pillar of support, my sister for all the cheering and my son for his creative inputs while designing the book.

Om Shree Swami Samarth

Contents

Foreword   *ix*

Preface   *xiii*

Acknowledgements   *xv*

1. Holiday Background – Choosing The Destination   1

2. Planning Singapore Itinerary, Tickets, Visas & Stay.   5
   Additional Tours - Ferry To Bintan Islands, Indonesia

3. Departure Day, T2 Check-in & Checking Out   10
   Mumbai Duty Free – Day Zero

4. Singapore Airlines Experience, Changi Arrival &   12
   Drive To Ymca – Day 1

5. Little India: Mustafa's, Indian Food & Ez Link Mrt   15
   Card – Day 1

6. Orchard Road: Gst Refund Via E-trs, Mall Hopping   19
   At Orchard Road, Singapore Visitor Centre & Ananda
   Bhawan – Day 1

7. Jurong Bird Park, Jurong Point Mall & Singapore   24
   Discovery Centre – Day 2

8. Downtown Core Walk: Cavenagh Bridge, Raffles   27
   Landing Site, Acm @empress Place, Padang,
   Esplanade, Merlion Park & Tekka Centre – Day 2

9. Botanical Gardens: Eco Lake, Foilage & Orchid   32
   Garden And Bee's Knees– Day 3

10. Mandai Wildlife: Singapore Zoo, River Wonders,   35
    Night Safari & Jaggi's North Indian Cuisine

Contents

Restaurant, Little India– Day 3

11. National Museum And Plaza Singapura – Day 4   40

12. Marina Bay: Sg Flyer, Cruise Centre, Racing Circuit, 42
Marina Bay Sands Shoppe, Artscience Museum,
Gardens By The Bay & Komala Vilas – Day 4

13. Chijmes, Raffles Hotel, Long Bar & Suntec City –   48
Day 5

14. Chinatown: Pagoda Street, Sri Mariamman Temple, 50
Buddha Tooth Relic Temple & Potato Head, Clarke
Quay, Boat Quay, River Cruise & Dining @ Harrys
–day 5

15. Fort Canning Park, Sentosa Island & Rws Hotels –   55
Day 6

16. Sentosa Sea Aquarium, Malaysian Food Street, Trick 58
Eye Museum, Sentosa Express Monorail & The Luge
Adventure – Day 6

17. Cable Car To Mt.faber, Vivo City Mall, Pangat   61
Restaurant, Sentosa Boardwalk Scenic Views &
Casino – Day 6

18. Universal Studios, Adventure Cove Waterpark &   66
Madamme Tussauds Sentosa – Day 7

19. Fort Siloso, Palawan Beach, Southern Most Point Of 69
Continental Asia, Tanjong Beach & Royal Taj
Restaurant – Day 7

Contents

20. Jewel Changi: Rain Vortex, Forest Valley & Canopy   73
Park, Changi Experience Studio And Gst Refund
Claim At Airport– Day 8

• vii •

Foreword

<u>Tamal Bandyopadhyay - award winning author &
columnist and an avid traveller</u>

When most of us were busy attending countless zoom meetings; reaching out for the pulse oximeter & digital thermometer every time we went out of home, for taking the pet out for a walk or buying vegetables; and watching Netflix for timepass during the pandemic, a banker chose to re-imagine a leisure international holiday by penning this book describing a couple's crystal wedding anniversary overseas trip with their teenage daughter.

The wife was behind the idea. During the 15 years of married life, the couple went overseas for holiday only once – to Mauritius. Two of them were there. Now they are three and the choices are very different – ranging from doing adventures to having a relaxed outing, laced with dollops of shopping. And, of course, they must have access to vegetarian Indian food.

Finally, as they were victims of the PMC Bank fraud —it will take years to get back their money kept in the form of fixed deposits in the cooperative bank which went belly up— it must be a "thrifty" international tour.

Banking on memory, million miles of virtual travel, reading and research, Ashiesh zeroed-in on Singapore for the holiday. This book, an outcome of that trip, attempts to bring alive the sights, sounds, flavours, and attractions of the lion city, 'Singa Pura' — the name unsurprisingly being of Sanskrit origin. The travel tale not only enlivens the cultural melting pot of Singapore but also celebrates the deep Indian connection. For instance, it captures Chennai's continued romance with the city-state, centuries after

Tamil traders pioneered the early Serangoon settlement in the early 19th century.

It reads more like a fiction than a traditional travelogue which entertains and, at the same time, is informative. It incorporates all the facts one needs to have on the table for sightseeing, shopping, eating out -- much like a Lonely Planet destination guide. And, the author has not missed out on anything important. The book discusses at length how the vegetarian family from Pune packed bhakarwadi, besan laddu, chiwda and shrewsbury biscuits in their check-in bags. With an eye for details, the author has effortlessly inter-woven the travel experience of a family where three members have different tastes and different expectations from the trip.

This book is not about MICE (meetings, incentives, conferences and exhibitions) travel or corporate travel. It focusses on leisure and aims at drafting a blueprint for the aspiring Indian middle-class tourist to design a relaxed Singapore vacation which is affordable and free from the stresses of rigid touch-and-go tours. Probably it will inspire the tour agencies to redesign their packages, making them more comfortable and affordable for the deserving desi travellers.

The narrative focusses on the peculiar needs and characteristics of an aspiring Indian traveller. Desi food finds top priority in the overall scheme of things. The sweets and savouries, meticulously chosen by the Punekar family for their Singapore-based friends, are warmly reciprocated by delicious traditional vegetarian fare dished up by their buddies. The book diligently encapsulates North and South Indian cuisine eateries across the Orchard, Serangoon Road & Sentosa Island for the fussy traveller; the must-try Singapore street food at Chinatown and Little India for the adventurous lot; and the Clarke Quay river-side restaurants for an authentic local dining experience which is not complete till you choose your crab and the sauce to go with it!

In an otherwise well-researched and well-told travel book, that aims at helping design a classy yet pocket-friendly trip, one thing is missing – tips for resource allocation. While multiple choices for hotels and flights have been discussed and their impact on the cost of the tour is dissected with precision, it could have done well by giving an idea of the overall cost of a week's trip in Singapore for a family. For instance, the rack rates for different kinds of accommodation to choose from – across budget, premium and luxury hotels – would have added value and come in handy for those who would plan a trip to the island nation after reading the book. Of course, backpackers and well-heeled guests visiting paid or free attractions explore a country, however small or big, differently and seek different experiences. This makes the budget forecasts as difficult as a central bank's inflation estimate!

To the book's credit however, there are clues galore to save money when Indian tourists are busy with the obligatory shopping rituals, typically pushed and nudged by the womenfolk – how to get the GST refund for applicable goods in Singapore as well as ways to secure discounts and deals. Must visit places are neatly tabulated for the reader's benefit.

The author has set the trip in January 2020 just before the pandemic erupted but he has not forgotten to add things which one needs to know if they want to pack their travel tool kit now. I will wait for his next travel book which might come few years later when the protagonist couple celebrates their porcelain anniversary!

Preface

Being a seasoned corporate banking veteran of Global Trust, BNP Paribas, FirstRand Bank and L&T Financial Services, I have had the privilege of travelling for work and leisure across Africa, Europe & Asia including Singapore. Given my extensive banking background, I have also written opinion pieces in reputed Indian financial dailies, with my Op-ed articles having been featured in the Financial Express, HT Mint and the Hindu Business Line.

Business and leisure travel to SG on multiple occasions has helped me cultivate a healthy understanding of the heritage, customs, ethos and everyday life in the cultural melting pot of Singapore.

ppp

Inspiration behind writing the book - The pandemic induced lockdowns afforded me the opportunity to virtually re-discover super holiday destinations like Singapore once again, since physical travel was obviously out of bounds. This led to the idea of capturing important but lesser known ingredients and nuances of a SG holiday trip in the form of a fictional travelogue, that could potentially serve as a blueprint or a template for the aspiring Indian family and solo traveller, to design their own slow and relaxed, immersive Singapore travel experience. As international travel picks up post the pandemic, the book attempts to brings alive the sights, sounds, flavours and attractions of the lion city, Singapura.

True Bird Paradise - Amongst parakeets at the Jurong
Bird Park, Jurong

Acknowledgements

I wish to express my sincere gratitude to the Singapore Tourism Board (STB) India team specially Jay Bhavsar, the team at Resorts World Sentosa (RWS), helpful folks at YMCA @ 1 Orchard Road, the Mandai Wildlife Group, Singapore Airlines and the publishing team for information and/ or feedback on specific queries. Will like to specially thank Tourism Information & Services Hub (TIH) website and STB for access to their pictures used in this SG travel book celebrating Singapore as well as Notion Press for images used on the cover pages.

Grateful to Shri Tamal Bandyopadhyay, award winning author and respected columnist, for graciously agreeing to pen the book's Foreword and providing a splendid introduction to my first travel book. Heartfelt thanks to industry globetrotters - M/s. Mohit Agarwal, Kedar Lele, Rajat Sinha, Amita Trehan and Manish Mathur for taking the time out to provide their thoughtful reactions, duly incorporated as comments on the book's back cover.

A quick shout-out also to my extended family, colleagues, friends and all Visit Singapore enthusiasts who've directly or indirectly provided the inspiration and encouragement in compiling this SG holiday travelogue.

ONE

Holiday Background – Choosing the Destination

Travel has been spoken about and practiced as an art since many centuries. This conviction offered little comfort to Aditya Kumar, an executive at European bank in Poona, who was caught in a dilemma when his wife, Jyoti suggested celebrating their crystal wedding anniversary abroad. While he had occasionally travelled on official work across Asia, an international family holiday was quite foreign to them.

Jyoti, a self-employed marketing professional, had not travelled to foreign shores for ages other than a visit to Mauritius after their marriage. Being a vegetarian, international cuisine found little favour with her fussy taste buds. Castigated by Jyoti's mother for her fasting ways and weight loss post their Mauritius honeymoon, they had taken a decision to restrict holidays henceforth to desi food compliant domestic destinations.

Seeking a long overdue change, Jyoti however insisted on an overseas holiday to celebrate the special fifteenth anniversary in January 2020, along with their teenage daughter Yashika. The teenager was predictably over the moon hearing about her maiden voyage abroad. Of course, Yashika had another secret motive – giving destination feedback for a proposed educational tour planned during the school's summer break.

Putting their hidden gastronomical fears aside, Aditya and Jyoti began to plan finances for the foreign holiday. The PMC bank fraud unearthed recently was playing on their mind and like many other unsuspecting depositors lured by high PMC bank rates, the Kumars too had lost access to the sizeable locked up deposits. Nonetheless, figuring out that his employer's concessional overdraft facility can help bridge any funding shortfall, a triumphant smile soon settled on Aditya's face.

The cheer proved short lived though. Choosing the anniversary destination was no easy task, what with multiple competing choices. Jyoti looked forward to a relaxed, classical self-sightseeing tour while the teenage daughter was routing for an adventure cum beach holiday, that she could proudly record in her daily diary. The girls seemed to agree only on two things— the destination should be a shoppers' delight and offer plenty of Indian food options.

A trip to America or Europe needed months of planning to work out schedules in a pocket friendly manner and considering it was Diwali time already, flight and hotel fares had soared. Besides, the northern hemisphere winter could be quite severe. Considering this and keeping overall budget in mind, US and Europe as ports of call were dropped. Looking closer home, Maldives, UAE and Ceylon largely met expectations on the cuisine, culture and budget counts but the family was looking for the elusive X-factor to make their holiday special.

After much deliberation, the family shortlisted two locales situated either side of Malacca Straits – Singapore and Phuket. Singapore city-state that extends all of 280 square miles, fitted the bill perfectly not only for its multitude of gardens, museums, adventure activities, shopping arcades and exceptional sight-seeing hotspots, but also for its welcoming warm equatorial climate that makes it an all-year round destination. Yet, what provided the wow-factor and clinched the deal in favour of Singapore was its alluring aura as a cultural melting pot and the famed cosmopolitan architecture.

The family's other key aspiration was undertaking a self-exploratory holiday over a decent length of time. The Kumars' preferred a relaxed, slow immersive travel experience that balanced their itinerary with a languid pace providing ample time to explore more and eliminating the stress of rushing around many places to tick all boxes. Travelling in time constrained customised trips was not their cup of chai. The family yearned for the thrill of exploring the unknown by themselves, albeit in an organised, well researched manner.

Strenuous morning to night group travel schedules or boring touch & go tours certainly wasn't their idea of a vacation either. Moreover, Jyoti remembered her widely travelled brother's rather underwhelming gourmet experience while travelling on a reputed group tour to Singapore, where he survived three full days only on biryani! During another visit, while her cousin faced lesser issues having gone in for a customised four day SG trip, it still lacked the thrill of a self-exploratory overseas holiday and happiness that flows from freedom to explore places at your own pace.

With the anniversary destination now locked in, the Kumars set about the task of planning out the air tickets and stay details for their Singapura staycation sojourn. While Aditya was familiar with the geography having travelled on work in the past, Jyoti knew much more given her active social media presence and heterogeneous friend circle.

TWO

PLANNING SINGAPORE ITINERARY, TICKETS, VISAS & STAY. ADDITIONAL TOURS - FERRY TO BINTAN ISLANDS, INDONESIA

The art of thrifty international air travel demands booking tickets many months in advance and usually through a single airline, for both onward and return flights. But the family's travel program to Singapore was drawn up rather late in the day, which necessitated looking at multiple combinations.

Flight Schedule

After a quick search, Jyoti ascertained that Indigo and Scoot offered great deals but offered limited pricey meal options onboard. Realizing that bored children blindly ape fellow airline passengers to order spartan food-packs at absurdly priced gourmet fine-dining rates, Jyoti wisely decided to evade in-flight embarrassment and pay extra upfront to savour the legendary hospitality of Singapore Airlines for the onward journey. Moreover, SIA's early morning arrival at Changi airport meant an entire day for taking in the city sights.

The home leg of Singapore- Mumbai was also crucial as the intention was to take as late a flight out as possible and have ample time left for exploring the fabulous Jewel Changi airport attractions. While there were airlines offering cheaper mid night connections to Mumbai via brief stopovers, the family settled for a late evening Air India direct flight which also guaranteed them a hot desi maharajah meal at the end of a long day.

Once the flight selections were frozen, realizing that there was hardly any difference between travel website prices of Make My Trip/ Go Ibibo/ airline website and offline travel agent quotes, the Kumars went ahead with the online site air tickets and insurance bookings.

Currency

The Kumars arranged the forex primarily in US Dollars (USD) with a small quantum of Singapore Dollars (SGD) in pre-paid forex card and smaller cash denomination, as they felt need-based USD-SGD conversion could be done easily at the destination.

Visas

The Singapore E-Visa application was filled and submitted to an authorised visa agent, well prior to the thirty days of arrival timeline. With documents being in order and the tourist visa fee of S$30 per person paid besides a small agent fee, the Singapore E-Visa printout was easily arranged by the authorised agent within ten days' time.

Hotels

Given the multitude of tourist sightseeing, shopping and dining options in the downtown core of Singapore, the location was of paramount importance in deciding the hotel. Jyoti and Aditya pursued various hotel options across the premium, mid-scale and economy hotel categories.

Realty in the tiny city state can be expensive and so the hotel selection, especially for longish stays, had to be well thought through. Planning to spend 7 nights and 8 days in Singapore, the Kumars split the stay into two parts – the first 5 night stay at an affordable executive economy or midscale property in downtown Singapore and for their anniversary, the last 2 nights at a premium resort in Sentosa.

For the bulk of their stay in downtown hub, they considered various superior hotels including 4-star properties like Orchard hotel and Novotel on Stevens, the latter offering free lodging & breakfast to children under 16 years, as well as good 3-star properties like Ibis hotel at Bencoleen and Holiday Inn Express near Orchard Road & Clarke Quay.

Yet, considering the location and excellent reviews from people around the world, the choice was not difficult to make. YMCA @ 1 Orchard Road perfectly fitted the requirement of a quality, affordable accommodation in the city centre. The 3-star hotel is conveniently located in downtown core close to Fort Canning Park, National Museum of Singapore, Singapore Management University, Little India quarter, Raffles, Padang, Esplanade Park and the key shopping boulevard of Orchard Road.

For celebrating their anniversary, Jyoti was keen on staying in a swanky yet not overtly expensive hotel in Sentosa Island, where they could spend the day checking out the beautiful attractions, beaches and adventure activities before retiring to one of the plush hotels. Sentosa is home to many hotel properties like the Shangri La, Sofitel and Capella hotel that hosted the 2018 summit meeting of US president, Donald Trump and North Korean leader Kim Jong-un. But considering its integrated facilities, attractions and choice of five hotels to choose from, Jyoti chose the Resorts World Sentosa for their special occasion.

Jyoti and Aditya were hopeful that the luxury stay and activity bouquet at Resorts World Sentosa during their last two nights in Singapore would offer them an experience of a lifetime comparable with the iconic Dubai hotel property - Atlantis, The Palm Resort.

Consider Ferry trip to Indonesian Islands

Enterprising Indian tourists and foreigners having the luxury of additional nights to spare, can also better leverage their Singapore air travel spends by hopping on to regular ferries to the Indonesian island resorts of Bintan and Batam, which are only 60-to-90-minute boat ride away from the city's ferry terminals at Harbourfront or the one near Changi.

Depending on the nationality and visit purpose, travellers can commute visa-free or simply avail the visa on arrival facility. Bintan island, which has plenty of forests, beaches, golf courses and affordable luxury resorts, is being developed as a major tourist centre next only to Bali.

Many Indian tourists also like to combine a trip to Malaysia, easily accessible by road via the Johor Bahru causeway and by air from Changi. This however requires arranging a Malaysian visa beforehand. The Kumars decided to restrict their stay to Singapore this time around.

THREE

DEPARTURE DAY, T2 CHECK-IN & CHECKING OUT MUMBAI DUTY FREE – DAY ZERO

On the D-Day in Poona, Jyoti oversaw the last-minute formalities. Their anxiety over quality care for the adorable floppy-eared, snow-white Shih Tzu, Leo was well resolved as their cousin, Happy – an ardent dog lover had volunteered to nurture the family's favourite pet.

Jyoti inspected the packed bags that included popular desi snacks for their Singapore based friends. She securely tucked in Chitale's bhakarwadi & besan ladoos, Laxmi Narayan chiwda, Buddhani wafers, Mapro's ghee khakra, whole strawberry jam and mazaana milk chocolates along with Kayani's ginger & shrewsbury biscuits.

After a post lunch nap and early tea, they zoomed their way across the expressway in an uber cab straight to Mumbai's T2 international airport. Having reached well in time for their midnight flight, the Kumars leisurely checked-in their baggage at the Singapore Air counter.

Expectedly, their bags had plenty of spare storage capacity to accommodate the planned shopping purchases. Security check and emigration too were routine affairs and didn't take much long. They made it a point to declare the foreign currency and gadgets being carried, to avoid any issues with Customs on their return.

Thereafter, Jyoti and Yashika dutifully visited the Mumbai duty-free to check out the perfume collection. Taking the cue, Aditya also enthusiastically surveyed the prices of single malts and select brands, to see if he would get a better deal at the Mumbai duty-free on return or consider buying in Singapore. At the appointed hour, the family proceeded to board their flight and were welcomed by warm smiles of the smartly dressed cabin crew of Singapore Airlines.

FOUR

SINGAPORE AIRLINES EXPERIENCE, CHANGI ARRIVAL & DRIVE TO YMCA – DAY 1

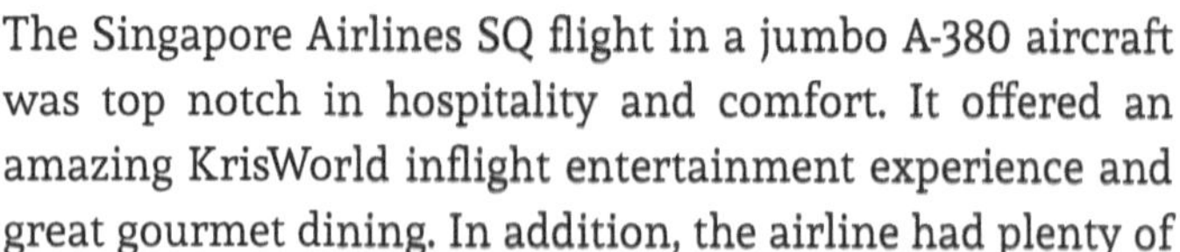

The Singapore Airlines SQ flight in a jumbo A-380 aircraft was top notch in hospitality and comfort. It offered an amazing KrisWorld inflight entertainment experience and great gourmet dining. In addition, the airline had plenty of variety in their meals and served a wide array of beverages.

Jyoti enthusiastically opted for the famed Singapore Sling cocktail – a mix of dry gin, cherry brandy and orange liqueur with a dash of lime, pineapple juice and grenadine. Aditya was content with a glass of his favourite Scotch while Yashika enjoyed her Golden Dawn mocktail of pineapple, tomato and orange juice. This was followed by a sumptuous meal of their choice. After viewing their choicest movies from KrisWorld's expansive program library, it was time to catch up on sleep. Post a decent nap, morning tea and snacks served by the cheerful air hostesses made for a delicious breakfast.

With clockwork precision, the SQ flight landed smoothly at Changi's PTB3 terminal at its scheduled time early Wednesday morning. The immigration was quick and a straight forward affair. In half an hour, the Kumars had completed the formalities and collected their baggage. They had three transport options for reaching their hotel – getting a taxi from PTB3 terminal itself, taking a MRT train service from level 3 of PTB2 terminal till Dhoby Ghaut Station or taking a bus from PTB2 basement that would drop them on the doorsteps of YMCA hotel @1 Orchard Road.

Given that they had arrived early and were well fed, they decided to take in the sights of Singapore streets via bus #36 which takes guests from the Airport to Orchard Road and originates every ten minutes from Changi terminal 2 basement. While they could use the inter-terminal travellators and the mezzanine level link bridge from PTB3 to reach PTB2 in minutes, they hitched a complimentary ride in the Skytrain airport service to reach terminal 2.

With Aditya carrying smaller denominated Singapore Dollars and loose change, they didn't have to swap their US Dollars at the pricey airport currency counter and decided to convert later in the city at good exchange rates. From the basement bus stop, it was a pleasant 55-minute ride in bus #36 and absolute value for money by a mile. It also afforded them an opportunity to get a first-hand idea of the major landmarks & establishments in the Singapore metropolitan area, before disembarking at the YMCA bus stop, right outside their hotel at 10 AM.

YMCA @ One Orchard Road is conveniently located in Singapore's central precinct. It is a vibrant, cosmopolitan place with guests from around the world, much like the cultural melting pot of Singapore. Considered a simple no-frills 3-star budget property, YMCA is a friendly family hotel in downtown core with excellent reviews for its clean comfortable air-conditioned rooms and junior suites equipped with flat screen TV & refrigerator, signature cafe, a nice breakfast buffet spread, a fully functional gym and a big terrace pool with relaxing pool chairs lining its perimeter. Despite reaching early, the hotel check-in was a breeze although they had budgeted about an hour's waiting time. Dropping their baggage in their rather comfortable triple room and freshening up quickly, the family decided to explore what the city had to offer.

FIVE

LITTLE INDIA: MUSTAFA'S, INDIAN FOOD & EZ LINK MRT CARD – DAY 1

Being sedentary for much of the morning, the Kumars' proceeded to walk it down and explore the Little India quarter, less than a kilometre away. Bright colourful shops displaying their wares and people conversing in a familiar language greeted the family. Jyoti was reminded of the bazaars of Chennai and Bengaluru while walking down Serangoon Road, the main street of Little India.

Further ahead, Jyoti couldn't miss observing the busy hawker street-food activity and shops selling inexpensive wares at Tekka Centre. The large landmark, housed in a colourful warehouse, also serves up large dishes of fresh vegetarian and non-vegetarian food to visitors and locals, just steps away from the Little India MRT station. On a quick survey, she noticed hawker shops offering veg appam stew, stuffed pancake, Singapore soup noodles, biryani, omelette roti, smoothies, fresh tender coconut and desserts, to customers in search of decent food experience at honest prices.

After a brisk 20-minute walk from YMCA, they reached the gigantic Mustafa Centre. Whilst multiple money changers are available across the city, Aditya believed Mustafas was amongst the best in terms of rates across currencies. Promptly converting forex funds into local SGD, the Kumars decided to take lunch early. The plethora of Indian restaurants enroute including Komala Vilas, Kailash Parbat, Khansama Tandoori and Adyar Ananda Bhavan had vetted their appetite. The family settled for tiffin and mini meal at MTR restaurant near Mustafas.

Post a hearty meal, they were briefly tempted to spend the day at the Mustafa Centre mall. Aditya recounted the deep fascination his colleagues had for the iconic shopping centre. During a whirlwind Singapore trip years ago. Aditya vividly recalled accompanying his Chennai workmate to the Mustafas. The extended hanging around there brought back childhood memories of the long waiting periods at Nallis & Kumaran Silks whenever Aditya's mum and sister went hunting for the latest Kanjeevaram sarees. Years later, it dawned that his colleague's hours of shopping were well spent in selecting the latest Swiss watch and gifts for her fiancée. No wonder that a warm Madras relationship continues to have a sweet Singapore connection, centuries after Tamil traders pioneered the Serangoon settlement in early 19th century.

Recalling this experience and apprehensive of being stuck for the entire afternoon at Mustafas, Aditya deftly shepherded the family towards the next destination at Orchard. Besides, they could always visit Mustafa Centre post dinner as it was open 24 hours.

Enroute, the Kumars bought some bottled water and fruit juices from a nearby 7-eleven store. Whilst walking around is the best way to explore Singapore, perspiration under the tropical afternoon sunshine warrants that fluids and deos are a must carry item in tourist backpacks here. At the Farrer Park MRT station, the Kumars purchased the Ez- Link CEPAS electronic money cards, that allows usage across MRT trains, Singapore buses, Sentosa express monorail and partner merchants. The smart card is extremely handy for tourist travel for longish stays and can be topped-up multiple times.

Tourists staying for shorter periods and not going in for Ez Link cards for MRT or bus travel, can also leverage their Singapore Airlines boarding pass for buying an unlimited one-day pass on special SIA Hop-On buses at discounted rates. These Hop-On buses have frequent services to key SG attractions across its original brown line, blue line, yellow city line and red heritage line routes. Singapore Airlines boarding pass privileges is being replaced by a new lifestyle rewards mobile application called Kris+ app from end 2020, bringing benefits across retail, dining and attractions. KrisFlyer members flying on an economy ticket from India will earn about SGD15 each in credit, which they could use post touchdown in Singapore. Moreover, customers purchasing SQ air tickets can utilise the proposed new Singapore Airlines online curated travel platform – Pelago from 2021, to browse through latest promotions as well as leverage discounts up to 50% across scores of Singapore attractions.

Young Yashika, meanwhile was most impressed by her first MRT ride and the seamless metro interchange to their destination, Somerset station on Orchard Road.

SIX

ORCHARD ROAD: GST REFUND VIA E-TRS, MALL HOPPING AT ORCHARD ROAD, SINGAPORE VISITOR CENTRE & ANANDA BHAWAN – DAY 1

Orchard Road, the prime promenade and shopping boulevard in Singapore, is easily accessible from the

Somerset Station, Dhoby Ghaut and Orchard MRTs. The girls marvelled at the impressive sights of the malls and arcades on either side of the shopping street – an absolute tourist delight. There are enough and more malls in Singapore city, easily in excess of a hundred, that can baffle any visitor.

When an overseas tourist shops for over SGD100 at participating shops, shoppers can claim refund of the current 7% GST paid on applicable purchases, while departing Singapore under the tourist refund scheme (TRS). Tourists need to look out for a 'tax free' shopping logo or signboard of central refund agency and carry their passports while out shopping. In fact, tourists are entitled up to three same-day receipts/ invoices from shops bearing the same GST registration number and shop name, to meet this minimum purchase amount of SGD100. The GST refund, post deduction of a small processing fee, acts as a welcome feel-good present while leaving Singapore.

Having done thorough research like any switched-on travelling tourist, Jyoti was aware about this vital shopping tip and the need to show passport to the retailers on electronic TRS while purchasing goods. Retailers issue an e-TRS transaction at the point of purchase that stores passport-wise shopping details in a centralized system. While exiting the country, travellers can visit the e-TRS self-help kiosks, before departure immigration in the airport departure check-in hall (purchases in check-in luggage) and after departure immigration in the departure transit lounge (hand baggage), for scanning their passports in the kiosks. The kiosk machine counterchecks shopping data and intimates if the passenger is required to present these goods physically at customs inspection counter for validation.

Armed with their passports and animated zest, the girls started their shopping quest with perfumes at seemingly bargain prices in Takashimaya shopping centre. Later, they looked for purses, apparel and bags at Tangs Plaza, Paragon centre, Orchard shopping centre and Orchard Central besides buying cosmetics from Concorde shopping mall. The Kumars also took time out to briefly step into the Singapore Visitor Centre near Orchard Gateway. It is a single stop touch-point which offers maps, sale of arts & entertainment tickets, electronic display of tours and attraction vouchers. Having their passports on person, they picked up some cute souvenirs from the retail outlet.

After the lightning shopping strike, the Kumars stopped by for some coffee at Starbucks in Plaza Singapura shopping centre. Starbucks was an old favourite with Aditya and his bank colleagues for over a decade. Their hands full with the day's catch, the trio quickly headed to their 1 Orchard Road hotel from Plaza Singapura, only a 5-minute walk away.

Dumping their shopping bags, it was time for choose a restaurant for dinner. While Awadh Royal Indian Dining is a lovely Lucknowi restaurant conveniently located at the Centrepoint shopping mall on Orchard Road, the Kumars opted for a South Indian traditional sapad meal at Ananda Bhawan in Little India quarter. Post dinner, time was well spent exploring and window shopping at the colossal Mustafa Centre.

It was past 11PM when they reached the hotel and hit the bed, after an eventful first day at Singapore.

<u>Yashika's Diary – Tourist Tips</u>

1. Stay

Choose comfortable, centrally located hotels close to MRT station, Bus interchange and within the city's downtown core

2. Transport

Ez link, smart travel cards are very convenient for MRT/ Buses & save time.

3. Orchard Road

A stroll on shopping street is a wonderful experience that rivals Champs- Elysees in Paris, London's Oxford Street or New York's Fifth Avenue

4. Surprises

Go to Singapore Visitor Centre for latest attraction information, gifts & promotions

5. Essentials

For replenishing any essentials like water or deos, step into the nearest Watsons or 7-eleven store

ᐳᐳᐳ

Mustafa Centre under festival lights, Little India (Top)
and Orchard Road near Tangs Plaza (bottom)

SEVEN

Jurong Bird Park, Jurong Point Mall & Singapore Discovery Centre – Day 2

Given the rather long first day in Singapore, a good night's rest was most welcome. Yashika was thankful for not having to get up at 5.30 AM on day2, which is usually the norm during many guided group tours. After enjoying a hearty English buffet breakfast at the YMCA, the Kumars headed to explore the famous bird park located in Singapore's western suburb of Jurong.

Taking a train from the nearby Dhoby Ghaut MRT station, they effortlessly changed from North South line to East West line at City Hall and reached Boon Lay MRT within 45 minutes. From the nearby bus interchange, they swiped their Ez link cards on bus #194 which took them straight to the destination.

Jurong bird park, run by Mandai group, is amongst the world's largest bird parks and hosts multiple bird species including endangered ones. As the Kumars planned visiting other big-budget Mandai wildlife attractions too, they bought a comparatively less expensive multi-park ticket called 4-in-1 park hoper pass that included admission and tram rides at Jurong Bird Park, Night Safari and Singapore Zoo as well as Amazon River Quest ride at River Wonders Safari.

At Jurong, the girls were mesmerized by the South American rainforests, penguin coast, African treetops, flamingo lake, watching the feeding sessions in the pelican cove, close encounters with the multi-colour parakeets in the walk-in aviary and different bird shows. They skipped the Songbird terrace, a pricey parrots show along with Asian buffet lunch comprising few vegetarian dishes.

Spending about two and a half hours at the bird park, it was time to take the bus back. Alighting at Boon Lay bus interchange, the family headed for McDonald's at the nearby Jurong Point Mall for a quick snack. From Boon Lay MRT, they took a short train ride to next door Joo Koon, the last station on the East West line.

The next destination high on Yashika's bucket list was the Singapore Discovery Centre (SDC) at Upper Jurong road, a 10-minute walk from the Joo Koon MRT. Although multiple experiences are available at SDC that's branded as an edutainment centre, Yashika was focussed on viewing the art exhibits gallery and science museum, that visually showcase Singapore's journey from past to the present. They also liked the display of aircraft outside the centre.

Returning to Joo Koon after spending an hour at SDC, they boarded the train to Raffles Place MRT which offered them an opportunity to relax during the 35-minute ride. Raffles Place MRT station in Singapore's downtown core is situated directly underneath the financial district of Raffles Place, the One Raffles Place shopping mall and the Raffles Place Park lawns. Raffles landing site across the Cavenagh Bridge and Asian Civilisation Museum were the family's next port of call.

EIGHT

Downtown Core Walk: Cavenagh Bridge, Raffles Landing Site, ACM @Empress Place, Padang, Esplanade, Merlion Park & Tekka Centre – Day 2

Exiting the Raffles Place MRT station, the Kumars strolled past the sculptures at Boat Quay and the scenic Cavenagh Bridge- a historical 19th century cable stayed suspension bridge for pedestrians. Crossing to the north bank of Singapore river, with views of the bum boats and imposing Fullerton hotel, they stopped by at the Raffles' Landing site – a statue and plaza devoted to the British East Indian administrator and Singapore city's founder, Thomas Stamford Raffles. Clicking pictures galore enroute, the family then quickly proceeded to their next destination, Empress Place - which is actually only a 7-minute walk from the MRT.

The classical Empress Place Building hosts the Asian Civilisations Museum (ACM) that showcases the artistic heritage of Asia, with display of relic collections of South East Asia, Indian subcontinent, Middle East, Chinese and Singaporean culture. After spending an hour at the ACM, it was almost 4.30 PM when they walked across the Empress Place lawns to the famous Padang fields or plains.

Padang has hosted many historic national events with the nearby Cenotaph at Esplanade Park being a famous war memorial. Crossing the Queen Elizabeth Walk, the trio strolled past the impressive Theatres on the Bay performing arts complex at Esplanade towards Marina Square Mall for some coffee.

Walking past the Esplanade, Aditya recounted his stay at the nearby Mandarin Oriental hotel during his first Singapore trip and the path traversed daily to reach the Collyer Quay offices. The month-long training at European bank offered Aditya ample opportunity to explore the

Garden City besides being introduced to the popular local cuisine at lunch eateries across the Quay.

After a fleeting rendezvous with Esplanade, the Kumars enthusiastically crossed the scenic Jubilee pedestrian pathway along the bridge to the Merlion Park, located on the south bank of Singapore river's mouth. The centre of attraction here is the famous Singapore tourist landmark and mascot, the Merlion – statue of a mythical creature with a lion's head and the body of a fish.

The Kumars had a great time soaking in the warm experience of orange skies and the sun setting against the waters of Merlion park. Yashika captured the precious moments in her camera before the family merrily trudged back via the Singapore river walk to the Raffles Place MRT.

While the initial intent was to proceed to Bugis MRT for checking out tech products at Sim Lim Square, growing hunger pangs lead to a last-minute change of plans. They proceeded instead to the Little India on way to their dinner destination, Tekka Centre.

The Kumars were amazed looking at the many shops and fresh sea food stalls in the Tekka Centre building. At the ground floor hawker centre, they encountered stalls selling Indian vegetarian and non veg dishes besides Malay and Chinese food. Aditya and Yashika feasted on the omclette rotis and Singapore soup noodles while famished Jyoti remained content with veg pancake and appam stews. Post dinner, they returned to the hotel tired but contented.

Yashika's Diary— Tourist Tips

1. Combo ticket

Consider combo tickets for savings when visiting big budget attractions

2. Fast food

When craving for a quick bite, head to any shopping mall basement where food courts are generally located, unlike the top floor in most Indian food courts

3. Singapore Street food

Best experienced at various hawker centres in China Town and at the Tekka Centre outside Little India MRT station, off Serangoon Road

4. Commuting essentials

Carrying a camera with spare capacity is most handy to capture the many memorable moments and so are deodorants or perfumes under the warm Singapore sunshine

❧❧❧

Merlion Park (Top) and Esplanade Theatres by the Bay
& Singapore river (bottom)

NINE

Botanical Gardens: Eco lake, Foilage & Orchid garden and Bee's knees– Day 3

Day 3 in Singapore was reserved exclusively for nature and wildlife – Botanical Gardens, River Wonders Safari, Singapore Zoo and Night Safari. Post an early hearty breakfast at the Y, the Kumars took a train from nearby Dhoby Ghaut MRT to Newton on the north south line and then conveniently changed to the downtown line, reaching Botanical Gardens MRT in 20 minutes. From the Botanical

Gardens MRT, the Bukit Timah gate of the Singapore Botanical Gardens is only a few metres away.

Besides the Botanical Gardens and Mandai attractions, nature lovers can also plan a trip to the 163-hectare Bukit Timah Nature Reserve that's accessible from Beauty World MRT on the downtown line. It is not only the oldest and largest forest reserve in Singapore but also the host of many hiking trails, rock climbing and mountain biking besides being the home of almost half of the Country's flora and fauna. The Kumars had kept this nature reserve as a back-up visit venue in case they had spare time left during the trip.

Founded in 1859, the 80-hectare Botanical Gardens managed by National Parks Board (NParks), is a UNESCO world heritage site and can be reached quickly from Orchard Road if one is travelling by car. Nparks also manages the recent vintage Coney Island Park at Punggol in North East Singapore which is home to coastal forests, mangroves and grasslands besides being popular for camping.

Singapore Botanical Gardens is accessible through multiple entrances – Nassim gate, Tanglin gate & Tyersall Gallop gate, which are great for parking one's car and Bukit Timah gate if taking the MRT. While many attractions in the Botanical Gardens are closer to Nassim gate, it entails a long walk to reach the entrance and so the Kumars found it better to enter through the gate adjacent to MRT and then walk inside the gardens exploring various sites therein.

The family checked out the black swans at Eco lake, bamboo collection, fruit trees, foliage garden, herbs & spices, Evolution garden and the famous national Orchid garden. Yashika keenly took notes as well as pictures of a variety of rare plants and flowers for her school biology project. Some cool refreshments at Bee's knees at the Garage point in the gardens was a welcome break.

After spending about two and a half hours, they headed back to the MRT towards their next destination at Mandai lake road. The journey to Khatib MRT on North South line via the Bishan exchange on Circle line, took about 25 minutes. Outside Khatib MRT station, they boarded a loop shuttle bus service called Mandai Express that took them 15 minutes to reach the Singapore Zoo coach bay post noon.

TEN

MANDAI WILDLIFE: SINGAPORE ZOO, RIVER WONDERS, NIGHT SAFARI & JAGGI'S NORTH INDIAN CUISINE RESTAURANT, LITTLE INDIA– DAY 3

Mandai wildlife group operates three attractions in close vicinity, viz Singapore Zoo, River Wonders Safari and Night Safari that opens after the zoo closure time. A fourth attraction named Bird Paradise is expected to come up in the same area late in 2022 where birds from the Jurong Bird Park are to be relocated while a fifth attraction named Rainforest Wild Park is likely to come up in 2024. This will make Mandai nature precinct a single integrated nature and wildlife destination in Singapore while helping reduce multiple location travel and hopefully, costs too for visitors.

The family lead by enthusiastic Yashika on the prowl decided to visit the Singapore Zoo first, which displays animals in naturalistic, open enclosures with hidden barriers and moats instead of metallic cages. They were amazed seeing the large colony of Sumatran orangutans, the African penguins, Californian sea lions, zebras, giraffes, kangaroos, Malayan flying fox, white tigers, and giant tortoise.

The zoo offers feeding sessions, paid personal buggy tour, private and discovery tours lasting an hour onwards. Yashika however was more interested in and had booked seats in advance for two 20-minute animal shows by trainers, viz rainforest fights back at the main amphitheatre and splash safari. Tired walking under the afternoon sun, they stopped by at KFC and café at the entrance for snacking and beverages. After three and a half hours at the zoo, it was time now for the River Wonders Safari.

River Safari's shaded river themed aqua zoo with freshwater exhibits and a river boat ride proved a welcome breather in the afternoon. The family were thrilled seeing the large panda exhibit and exotic creatures from different ecosystems like Africa's great river Nile, Brazil's Amazon and the Mississippi in USA. Attending the once upon a river show at the boat plaza was another highlight of the two hours plus trip.

After refreshments and bio breaks, the Kumars were at the gates of the Night Safari at 6.30PM. The tram ride alongside the animal enclosures was a pleasant experience whereby they could observe the nocturnal creatures from close quarters. There were a few walking trails as well like the fishing cat trail, wallaby trail and east lodge trail. They chose the leopard trail to see the big cats. The 25-minute creatures of the night show was also a big draw for the crowds at the amphitheatre.

Spending little more than two hours there, it was time to take the bus back to Khatib MRT and train thereafter to Little India station. Travelling by MRT during peak evening office hours from downtown core to the residential suburbs can pose an occasional challenge. During a MRT ride years ago from city centre to the Night Safari, Aditya's colleague Bawajee aptly compared the crowded yet orderly setting to a packed Valsad - Navsari bus ride. Luckily, the Kumars were travelling against the traffic in an empty train.

Post a power packed wildlife tour day, the family enjoyed a sumptuous tandoori roti, rajma and paneer meal at Jaggi's north Indian cuisine restaurant in Little India. Rejuvenated after a heavy dinner, it was time for some shopping at the gigantic Mustafa centre.

Besides replenishing their exhausted quota of juices and currency exchange, Aditya purchased some electronic and tech peripherals on his bucket list while Jyoti bought decorative articles, jewellery, souvenirs and a smart small polo bag to fit in the extra shopping spree goodies. Of course, they had their passports on them for the purposes of GST refund process. The Kumars also picked up some snazzy treats for Leo from the Pet Lovers store nearby. It was midnight by the time they trudged back to the hotel.

Yashika's Diary— Tourist Tips

1. Attraction reservation

Booking advance time slots at attractions can help save time, especially during holidays

2. Indian Food

For home food, visit desi restaurants in Little India

3. Mustafas

Shop till you drop and tick-off your bucket lists at the mammoth Mustafa Centre

ᗷᗷᗷ

Mandai Wildlife - Performers at Night Safari, Singapore Zoo (Top) and the River Wonders Safari (bottom)

ELEVEN

NATIONAL MUSEUM AND PLAZA SINGAPURA – DAY 4

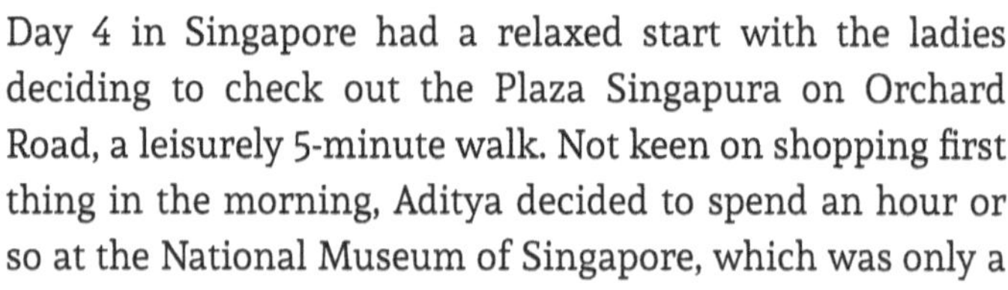

Day 4 in Singapore had a relaxed start with the ladies deciding to check out the Plaza Singapura on Orchard Road, a leisurely 5-minute walk. Not keen on shopping first thing in the morning, Aditya decided to spend an hour or so at the National Museum of Singapore, which was only a 2-minute stroll from the YMCA.

Singapore's oldest museum at Stamford Road houses both permanent galleries and periodic exhibitions. Aditya was impressed specially with the old-new world exhibition and history gallery that showcase Singapore's history from pre-colonial time to the present.

At the appointed hour, the family reunited at Plaza Singapura before heading out looking for bargains on batik textile, peranakan porcelain, Malay jewellery, miniature merlions, tiger balms and other souvenirs. Happy with the day's catch, the Kumars headed for east coast road township to meet their friends, Prasoonjit and family who were now based in Singapore.

Many Indian professional expats working in Singapore seem to be based out of the east coast colonies besides Newton. These colonies are close to the East Coast Park, that extends across 186 hectares and is the largest park in Singapore nesting predominantly on waterfront land.

Reaching the township, all the sweets and savouries from Chitale's, Kayani's and Mapro's being carried by the Kumars were offloaded and well received by their friends. The home cooked spread for lunch comprised shukto, shak, aloo posto, mishti doi and rosogollas. After the on-the-go munching during the past few afternoons, the Bengali favourites which are any vegetarian's delight back home came as a God-send gift, gratifying the taste buds of the yearning desi tourists. With their stomachs satiated, the group lead by the ladies was hungry to check out the lure of Marina Bay attractions.

TWELVE

Marina Bay: SG Flyer, Cruise Centre, Racing Circuit, Marina Bay Sands Shoppe, ArtScience Museum, Gardens by the Bay & Komala Vilas – Day 4

Post lunch, all of them drove down for a spin at the Singapore flyer- an attraction in Raffles boulevard near Promenade MRT in Marina Bay that comprises a terminal building and a giant observation ferries wheel with a diameter of 150 metres.

Yashika looked forward to the thrilling ride where visitors are transported on a 30-minute journey of stunning scenic views in the flyer's 28 fully airconditioned glass capsules. The spin did live up to their expectations except the 25-minute waiting time. They feasted on the bird's eye panoramic view of downtown Singapore in all its glory and noted the attractions they had already visited along with the unexplored sites. However, the Kumars missed out on the time capsule- a multisensory attraction of the city's heritage, culture and landscape - spanning two levels of the terminal building that Singapore flyer planned to launch in end 2020. The Kumars also learnt from their friends about proposed plans for a Museum of Ice creams in the garden city as well as anew 'garden-in-a-hotel', Park Royal Collection Marina Bay which would open in place of the erstwhile Marina Mandarin hotel in 2021.The latter would feature a 21-storey indoor skylit atrium, roof top gardens and more than 2,400 plants, trees and shrubs from 60 varieties of flora installed throughout the new hotel.

The families then drove across downtown bay that regularly hosts the Formula One motor car racing at Marina Bay Street Circuit, usually under the night sky. They also looked up the Marina Bay Cruise Centre, a modern deep-water centre that can accommodate some of the largest cruise liners popular with tourists keen on exploring South East Asia. Aditya's cousins were all praise for the Royal Caribbean 4-night cruise experience, which involved boarding at Marina Bay and day halts at Penang & Phuket, with itineraries and stopover visa arranged by the cruise team. Even overnight cruise experiences at the Marina Bay Cruise Centre are hugely popular with tourists to Singapore.

Later, they proceeded to the towers of Marina Bay Sands – a set of three skyscraper buildings connected at the top by a boat shaped park. Marina Bay Sands is an integrated resort with hotel complex, casino, celebrity chef restaurants, bars, night clubs, ArtScience museum building shaped like a lotus flower with exhibition galleries across its ten finger extensions, theatres, shopping mall and convention centre, which is located close to Bayfront MRT station in Marina Bay. Jyoti recounted that when her friends decided to celebrate their 10th anniversary by flying out to Singapore on a weekend sans kids, they were floored by the gorgeous infinity pool and the cool observation deck atop the iconic roof at Marina Bay Sands hotel.

Singapore is also one of the largest gaming markets in Asia Pacific region and the two casino operators – Marina Bay Sands along with Resorts World Sentosa enjoy a duopoly in the city state, with gaming being the bread-and-butter business of the integrated resorts.

Visiting the shoppes next at Marina Bay Sands was a phenomenal retail experience and the group spent hours window shopping, checking out the luxury brands and street style clothing labels at the mall. Shopping here also meant saving on the car parking charges.

Still carrying their passports, the girls grabbed great deals on their favourite perfumes, with the retailer duly noting the e-TRS transaction details needed for claiming GST refund at the airport. The women spoke animatedly and seemed to be in a different zone all together. The only other time Aditya recollected seeing a ladies' gang go ga-ga over driving a fab bargain was way back in the late 1980s when his mum and aunts boisterously flaunted their Sarojini & Lajpat Nagar deal exploits whilst the menfolk sported puzzled looks, bewildered by the swift shift in feminine mood.

After a quick coffee, the Kumars and their friends decided to explore the Gardens by the Bay close by. The Gardens by the Bay is a nature park spanning more than 100 hectares and comprises three waterfront gardens- Bay South, Bay East and Bay Central. The friends had a great time clicking loads of pictures here.

The main attractions were the OCBC Skywalk yielding good aerial garden views, Supertree Grove besides the two ticketed conservatories, Cloud Forest and the Flower Dome greenhouse. The group visited the Cloud Forest which was a paid entry but the indoor waterfall and the coinciding misting experience made the charges worthwhile. Thereafter they headed for the towering Supertree Grove near the Lilypond. By nightfall, it was time to savour the free Gardens by the Bay light show with its mesmerising display of colours.

Gardens by the Bay along with Jewel Changi are inexpensive yet breath-taking attractions that should rank high in the priority experience lists of backpackers as well as the well-heeled travellers during a Singapore vacation.

Thereafter, the families headed to Komala Vilas restaurant at Serangoon Road for feasting on ghee rawa dosas, butter tomato onion uthappams and parotta with korma. After a hearty meal, Prasoonjit and family bid the Kumars a warm goodbye while dropping them off at the YMCA.

<u>Yashika's Diary— Tourist Tips</u>

1. Spare day for languish pace

For an immersive and relaxed travel experience, a spare day helps avoid rushing around to tick all boxes, that are often a bane of many jam-packed group tours

2. Marina Bay and Gardens

Marina Bay and the beautiful Gardens by the Bay are a great place to spend an evening for all tourist travellers wanting to soak in an authentic SG adventure

3. Smart Shopping & GST refunds

Carry a passport handy while shopping for claiming GST cash/ credit card refunds while leaving SG, valid on same day shopping and a maximum of three bills of the same vendor that aggregate to at least One Hundred Singapore Dollars.

❦❦❦

Marina Bay Sands & ArtScience Museum (Top) and
Gardens by the Bay- Flower Dome & Cloud Forest
Conservatories towards the left and Supertree Grove on the
right (bottom)

THIRTEEN

CHIJMES, RAFFLES HOTEL, LONG BAR & SUNTEC CITY – DAY 5

Day 5 was the last day of Kumars in downtown precinct before they shifted hotels the next day. Walking out briskly from the YMCA, they crossed the Singapore Management University which is a publicly funded private university modelled on the lines of Wharton. Yashika looked on in awe as they walked past the renowned global city university campus that comprises six muti disciplinary schools hosting ten thousand students across bachelors, masters and PhD degree programs.

Progressing ahead, they reached their first destination, the historic Chijmes complex at Victoria Street. Originally functioning as a Catholic convent, the complex has since been restored as a restaurant, shopping and entertainment centre and hosts two national monuments- Chijmes hall and Cadwell house. It is worth a while to visit its beautiful courtyards and alfresco dining areas.

The renovated Raffles hotel is located barely some hundred metres away from Chijmes. Originally established in 1887, the iconic Raffles hotel was occupied by the Japanese in 1942 during the second world war before being reclaimed by the British in 1945. Its famous long bar where the national cocktail, Singapore Sling was invented, has now relocated to an adjoining centre, Raffles shopping arcade. The Kumars clicked some pictures against the backdrop of this national monument which has seen multiple renovations.

Moving ahead, they reached their next destination, Suntec City at Temasek boulevard after a 10-minute walk. It comprises shopping malls, restaurants, exhibition centre and conference convention centres at adjacent Raffles boulevard. After a rejuvenating walk around the world's largest fountain, Fountain of Wealth three times to soak in the positive 'qi' energy, the Kumars explored the one-stop shopping arcade and sky garden before catching a quick bite in its food court.

From the adjacent Promenade station, the family took a train to their next destination, Chinatown MRT on the downtown line and then proceeded on a walking tour through the maze of narrow roads dotting Chinatown.

FOURTEEN

CHINATOWN: PAGODA STREET, SRI MARIAMMAN TEMPLE, BUDDHA TOOTH RELIC TEMPLE & POTATO HEAD, CLARKE QUAY, BOAT QUAY, RIVER CRUISE & DINING @ HARRYS – DAY 5

Originally a home for Chinese immigrants, there are loads of souvenir and other tourist shops at Chinatown offering crafts, clothes and antiques at a bargain.

The Kumars shopped at the Pagoda Street for batik and were amazed by the scale of Chinatown food street & Chinatown complex, the largest hawker centre offering Singaporean street food at budget prices. Aditya and Yashika tried a few traditional desserts at the stalls which they found unique and tasty.

Later they visited the Chinatown heritage centre museum, the 19th century Sri Mariamman temple which is the first Hindu temple in Singapore and the majestic Buddha Tooth Relic temple of recent vintage. On the way back, they couldn't miss the prominent Potato Head landmark, a multi-story private dining house with a restaurant and bar.

Back at the Chinatown station, they took a short ride to the next stop on North East line, Clarke Quay MRT enroute their next destination, Clarke Quay Jetty. While one can take the Singapore river cruise from various jetties including Esplanade jetty, Promenade jetty, Fullerton jetty, Merlion Park and Bay Front South, a bum boat cruise from Clarke Quay jetty or Boat Quay is the most favoured.

Clarke Quay is a historical riverside quay or wharf located upstream from the river mouth and also the home of various river side cafes, restaurants and bars which add to its nightlife. The Kumars experienced an unforgettable evening boat ride with great views of the Singapore Parliament, Fullerton hotel and key attractions in the river valley road, Esplanade and Marina Bay precincts.

After an exhilarating 40-minute river cruise, they walked leisurely along the river side soaking in all the sights before crossing over to Boat Quay on the opposite bank. Boat Quay once used to be the busiest part of old Singapore port and is now a tourist attraction with picturesque views of the city's central business district and filled with a row of shop houses along the Singapore river.

With the skies getting ready for another glorious sunset show, the family made their way to the Harrys bar & dining close by for some Tiger beer and pizza. Entering the joint, Aditya was reminded of his previous encounter at Harrys decades ago with his colleagues. Realizing that decibels would rise when a bawa, punju and mallu competed to have a peg too many, he had forced them then to make a quick exit, lest their colourful philosophical banter brought the house down!

Clicking some of their final photographs at the downtown core, they walked on the riverside pathway to the Raffles Place MRT for a train to Farrer Park via Dhoby Ghaut interchange. From Farrer Park MRT, the Kumars stepped across to the City Square Mall food court for some refreshing sugarcane juice and tender coconut water. Thereafter the family proceeded to the nearby Mustafa centre for currency exchange and purchasing the last few remaining bucket list articles including the latest smart watch for their cool dude cousin Happy, before their planned move to Sentosa towards the end of their holiday trip.

Post the Mustafa visit, the family snacked on pav bhaji, bhaturas and chaat at the Kailash Parbat restaurant in

Little India, before retiring to their 1 Orchard Road hotel.

<u>Yashika's Diary— Tourist Tips</u>

1. Raffles Hotel & Long Bar

When visiting the historic Raffles hotel, take out time to savour the unique Singapore Sling at the famous Long Bar located closeby

2. Boating

Boating on Singapore river is an amazing way to take in the downtown core sights, specially at sunset

3. Chinatown

Exploring Chinatown markets & attractions on foot is a surreal experience

4. Dining at the Quay

Dining at the river side cafes, bars and restaurants at Clarke Quay and Boat Quay is a must do for tourists on a leisure holiday to Singapore

ᗡᗡᗡ

Clarke Quay-Dining & Boating (Top) and Buddha Tooth
Relic Temple- Chinatown (bottom)

FIFTEEN

FORT CANNING PARK, SENTOSA ISLAND & RWS HOTELS – DAY 6

On their final day at YMCA, the Kumars decided to go for a morning walk at the adjacent Fort Canning Park. While not as massive as the Hyde Park London or the Central Park New York, Fort Canning Hill Park spread over an area of 18 hectares is a similar downtown parkland, where the founder of modern-day Singapore, Sir Stamford Raffles had built his first home. This historic landmark was the place where the British surrendered to the invading Japanese during the Second World War and also the seat of Malay royalty that ruled in medieval era. The family enjoyed exploring the fort gate that includes remnants of a 19th

century fortress as well as the verdant spaces of the Fort Canning greens that's also a popular venue for stage and music concerts.

After their Monday morning breakfast and a quick shower at the hotel, they bid a fond goodbye to the Y which had hosted them for five full days. Grabbing a Grab taxi, they headed for their next destination, the gorgeous Sentosa Island by noon. Local Singaporeans often visit Sentosa to have a fun day out at the beach, partake adventure activities and explore its numerous attractions.

Jyoti had smartly sifted through the various luxury stay options at Sentosa before deciding to book a hotel at Resorts World Sentosa. Resorts World, run by Genting Singapore, has 5 upscale themed hotel properties in Sentosa itself to choose from – Festive hotel, Hard Rock, Equarius hotel, Crockfords Tower and Hotel Michael besides beach villas, tree top lofts and ocean suites.

To bring in their anniversary, they desired a classy 5-star hotel with spacious rooms and not necessarily the most uber luxurious. While Festive hotel is great for families offering sofa/ bunk beds and located in close proximity to many attractions, Crockfords Tower on the other hand is an exclusive all-suite luxury hotel with dedicated butler service at your beck and call.

Equarius hotel, nestled along the fringes of a tropical rainforest away from the hustle & bustle at the island, was the hotel Jyoti had eventually selected. Its spacious rooms and bathrooms, spectacular scenes of the forest / sea from the balcony, complimentary shuttle buggy rides and its lovely gardens with views of cable cars overhead helped the Kumars decide on the hotel for their two-night Sentosa experience.

Arriving in Sentosa a little post noon, the Kumars received a warm friendly welcome at the Equarius reception. Yashika was thrilled at being offered the popular American ice cream brand, Ben & Jerry's by the reception officer, who not only cheerfully facilitated an early check-in, but also clarified queries on the places of interest and advised reserving time slots at the popular attractions. Luckily for the Kumars, it wasn't very crowded being a regular week day.

Enjoying the pleasant buggy ride to their room, Jyoti was floored by the beautifully decorated deluxe room having a sit out balcony with eye-catching views besides the spotless washroom fitted with a bathtub.

SIXTEEN

SENTOSA SEA AQUARIUM, MALAYSIAN FOOD STREET, TRICK EYE MUSEUM, SENTOSA EXPRESS MONORAIL & THE LUGE ADVENTURE – DAY 6

Freshening up in the hotel quickly, the family proceeded to purchase Sentosa fun pass with tokens and proceeded to the S.E.A aquarium. The aquarium is a vast 20,000 square feet indoor aquarium that's home to over a hundred thousand marine animals of about 1,000 species, across 50 different habitats.

The family was awestruck the moment they stepped into the entrance tunnel with sharks swimming all around. The huge variety of marine life included squadrons of manta rays, magnificent leopard sharks, dolphins, jelly fish, eels and goliath groupers. The many marine ecosystems hosted aquatic species from the Straits of Malacca, Andaman Sea, Great Lakes of East Africa, coral reefs and cold-water habitats.

The centrepiece is the Open Ocean habitat, a gigantic aquarium making one feel as though you've dived into the depths of the big blue ocean floor and one can even sit in solitude on the benches facing the marine life. Yashika enjoyed the sea related activities for children as well as the free shows where divers feed the fish.

Having spent more than two hours at the S.E.A. aquarium, they headed to the nearby Malaysian food street situated outside Universal Studios. The hawker stalls here offered good food at cheaper prices and the family feasted on some noodles, pot rice, biryani and even roti chana. After a rather late lunch, they decided to visit the Trick Eye museum, located next door. This optical art museum from Korea houses funny & creative two-dimensional paintings and art works that appear not only as realistic 3D images but are brought to life through use of augmented reality technology. With no restrictions on touching or taking photographs, people can throw themselves into the exhibits displayed and click unforgettable pictures for posterity.

With the hot afternoon sun becoming more bearable, it was time to take a short walk to the Waterfront station, now called the Resorts World station. From there, they took a free ride on the Sentosa Express monorail towards the Beach station direction and got down at the next stop, Imbiah station. From Imbiah, it was another brief walk to their next destination, Skyline Luge. Sentosa Express, which starts from a shopping mall named Vivo City connected to Harbourfront MRT on Singapore's mainland, usually charges passengers for the ride into Sentosa island. The return trip for any tourist to Vivo City, irrespective of whether they entered the island via the monorail or not, is free and so is any amount of intra-island travel between Waterfront, Imbiah and Beach stations at Sentosa.

The Luge, also called toboggan, sleigh or sledge, offers a wheeled gravity ride downhill on custom built four luge tracks with tunnels, hairpin corners and exciting slopes on the descent. Once the luge ride downhill is complete, one can take the skyride back to the top and try another track trail. The Kumars especially Yashika was thrilled with the jungle trail luge cart experience and her photos on the luge cart, collected after the skyride back, aptly reflected her excitement.

SEVENTEEN

CABLE CAR TO MT.FABER, VIVO CITY MALL, PANGAT RESTAURANT, SENTOSA BOARDWALK SCENIC VIEWS & CASINO – DAY 6

The family moved ahead to the statue of Merlion Sentosa after the luge experience. A newer version of the original statue at Merlion Park in downtown core, the place nevertheless made for some lovely pictures.

Thereafter, they proceeded to the nearby Sentosa cable car station for a ride to Mount Faber and back to Harbourfront tower on the mainland. Jyoti was aware that visitors can experience two exciting independent cable car rides – Sentosa cable line running within the island across three stations namely Merlion, Imbiah lookout (which is a 5-minute walk from Mt. Faber line's Sentosa cable car station) and Siloso point. The other being the Mount Faber line which connects Sentosa island with Mt. Faber peak via the busy Vivo City/ Harbourfront station duo on the mainland.

The Kumars' cable car experience on the Mt Faber line was simply breath taking. The ride gave them panoramic views of the ships docked at Harbourfront and the Sentosa boardwalk, a 700-metre pathway across the channel that people can walk from Vivo City mall to Sentosa. Getting down at Mt. Faber peak, the Kumars were treated to a birds-eye view of the Keppel harbour, Sentosa island, CBD landmarks and Indonesian islands in the distance. Mount Faber Park stands at one end of the Southern ridges walk and counts amongst the highest points in Singapore. Walking around in the garden, they took pictures with the ship's bell of happiness, statue of another baby merlion and a fence with wishing bells tied all around. On the way back in Cable car, they deboarded at Harbour front by dusk time and took the modest walk to explore Singapore's largest mall, Vivo City.

The gigantic Vivo City is a complete retail and lifestyle destination with plentiful options suiting diverse requirements of the most fussy shopper or experience seeking traveller. The centre of the mall was covered with seasonal holiday decors and the Kumars found its plentiful phone chargers and free Wi-Fi very useful. Besides the Sentosa express that departs from level 3, there's additionally a sprawling food court on the same floor. However, yearning for some quality Indian food, the Kumars decided to proceed to Pangat restaurant at the basement level, where they relished the north Indian spread on offer.

After a heavy dinner, the Kumars proceeded outside Vivo City's eastern gates towards the Sentosa boardwalk. The elevated wooden platform with covered and open pathways, lined with flowers & trees, made for a great romantic way to take in the lights and sights of the ships docked while taking a leisurely 15-minute stroll to the island on the anniversary eve. Jyoti was captivated by the boardwalk's benches where one could sit staring at the scenic sights, food stalls to grab a quick bite as well as walkalators for ease of walking.

Heading to their room at Equarius hotel after the refreshing walk, Yashika was keen to catch up on some of the TV shows. With the night still being young, Aditya and Jyoti headed to check out the Resorts World Sentosa Casino.

Open only to adults with a dress code of smart casuals, the Casino offers free entry for foreigners on displaying their passports while locals need to pay an entry fee of SGD 150! Jyoti was apprehensive entering the huge facility where professional gamers spend hours trying out their luck at card games, roulette and slot machines. The ambience was relaxed with complimentary coffee and soft drinks flowing although smoking was common. With bet minimums seemingly high for some card games, not all of them seemed to be aimed at casual gamers. Jyoti tried her hand at one of the slot games and enjoyed the unique experience although she didn't lose or win anything big. With the clock approaching midnight, they quickly decided to retire for the day.

On reaching their hotel room, they were in for a splendid surprise. Young Yashika had co-ordinated with the friendly Equarius staff to beautifully decorate the room and organised for a lovely cake to bring in their special occasion. The parents were delighted by the thoughtfulness of their daughter and the family captured the memorable cake cutting moments in a video for posterity.

<u>Yashika's Diary — Tourist Tips</u>

1. Resorts World Sentosa, RWS

RWS offers ample choice in 5-star hotel properties with Equarius hotel & Festive hotel being most popular

2. Luge & SEA Aquarium

Must visit adventure and tourist attraction

3. Malaysian Food street

Hawker street in Sentosa island which offers good snacking choices to tourists at cheaper prices

4. Cable car to Mt Faber

The cable car ride affords breath taking views of the Keppel harbour and Sentosa

5. Vivo City

City state's largest mall with plentiful retail, lifestyle & restaurant options

6. Casino

Adults may experience a one-time visit for responsible gaming

ᏏᏏᏏ

Universal Studios Singapore (Top) and S.E.A Aquarium (bottom), courtesy Resorts World Sentosa

EIGHTEEN

UNIVERSAL STUDIOS, ADVENTURE COVE WATERPARK & MADAMME TUSSAUDS SENTOSA – DAY 7

The Kumars woke up early on their anniversary day and were surprised by the breakfast restaurant staff who presented flowers to the couple. After freshening up, they proceeded to the famed Universal Studios around its opening time. Since they planned to take water rides later in the day, they made the sensible decision to wear swimsuits under their casual outfits.

Universal Studios Singapore, USS is South East Asia's first Universal theme park offering more than 25 thrilling rides, shows and attractions across 7 themed zones –Hollywood, New York, Sci-fi city, Ancient Egypt, The lost world, Far far away and Madagascar. Each zone is largely based on movies or television characters and features their own attractions, meet & greet spots, restaurants, food courts and retail stores across the park.

There's so much to experience that one can spend the better part of the day at USS. With lesser waiting period at opening hour on weekdays, the family headed first for the 4 D transformer ride where wearing the 3D glasses, the visual effects plus motion seemed so phenomenally real.

Next on the agenda was the Battlestar Galactica- Human v/s Cylon, a pair of inverted blue and traditional seated red roller coaster. After the highspeed thrill and shrill roller coaster experience that's not for the fainted hearted, they walked across the park to take the customary photos with Transformer characters and also Shrek mascots at Far far away zone.

With the sun becoming stronger by noon, they refilled their bottles from the water coolers located around the park. The family visited the Discover food court & Oasis spice café near ancient Egypt zone for some masala tea after the girls had already feasted on Italian pizzas at Loui's NY pizza parlour in the New York zone. Close to the exit, the Kumars stopped by at the souvenir shop to buy some cute gifts.

Moving on, the family decided to spend the hot afternoon hours at the Adventure Cove waterpark.

Reaching the waterpark after a reasonable walk, they rented a small locker to keep their bag with outfits and gifts. While the waterpark offers many experiences like the high-speed duelling race rides, the rocket hydro-magnetic coaster ride, tidal twister and snorkelling with tropical fish in the reef, the Kumars chose to spend time just relaxing by the lazy river and splashing in the wave pool.

Coming out wet and refreshed from the short waterpark visit, they changed and collected their bags to proceed to the nearby Waterfront monorail station and took the Sentosa Express to the Imbiah. Sentosa has a variety of attractions to offer visitors looking for different experiences. Tourists not keen to spend time in the theme parks, can instead choose to spend additional hours hiking across the Imbiah trail, exploring Fort Siloso or across the three beautiful beaches in the island.

Alighting from the monorail, Aditya, Jyoti and Yashika headed to Madame Tussauds for soaking in the Ultimate film star interactive experience where one can act, dance or audition for a role and take pictures alongside life-like statues of Bollywood superstars. Although they missed the Spirit of Singapore boat ride through a fantasy tropical garden, they enjoyed the colourful Images of Singapore and close encounters at Marvel Universal with Captain Marvel, Thor, Spider Man, Black panther and Ant man.

Post the customary pictures, they took the Sentosa Express from Imbiah to the beach station.

NINETEEN

Fort Siloso, Palawan Beach, Southern most point of Continental Asia, Tanjong Beach & Royal Taj Restaurant – Day 7

Getting out from the monorail at the beach station, they first headed to the Siloso beach. With the sun being just right, they crossed the Siloso beach walk towards the sandy sea shore. The steady breeze and the cool waters were a perfect recipe for relaxing under the sunshine. They couldn't help but notice the variety of bars playing lively music dotting the beachfront and enjoyed snacking there.

Later, they proceeded briskly to the historic Fort Siloso which saw military action during the second world war's battle of Singapore between the invading Japanese and the retreating British. The museum that displays vintage artillery, is a must visit for its military history and visual WWII chronicles, the surrender chambers and prisoner of war camp.

Walking back from the fort, the Kumars decided to take the complimentary beach tram shuttle from Siloso beach towards Panjong beach and got off at the Palawan beach drop point. Palawan is the prettiest beach at Sentosa and popular amongst both locals and tourists.

Besides a leisurely beach stroll at Palawan, the family crossed the rope bridge to the islet that is called the southernmost point of continental Asia. Multi-storey observation decks offer tourists great views of the ocean beyond. Moving on to the Tanjong beach walk, they stopped to savour the magnificent sunset in the orange sky.

With the sun going down in the sea, the trio took a beach tram towards Siloso and disembarked for the wings of time music and light experience. The family thoroughly enjoyed the multi-sensory night show with colourful lights set against the seam lasers, water fountains and good 3D effects. The show ended at just the right time as it was getting late for dinner.

Jyoti had earlier planned to take the romantic City lights dinner cruise on Royal albatross, a tall ship with 4 masts and 22 massive sails, whose open decks would have given them majestic views of Singapore's southern islands of St. Johns and Lazarus. However, the luxury boat cruise service was running full and so the sailing experience was postponed for a future Resorts World Sentosa visit.

Instead, Jyoti booked a dinner table at the Royal Taj restaurant, a short distance away from the Casino. The North Indian ala-carte meal topped with desserts for their anniversary dinner was sumptuous. The family then made their way back to their cosy room at Equarius hotel. With the departure day at the doorstep, the Kumars spent an hour or so packing their belongings before calling it a day by midnight.

Yashika's Diary— Tourist Tips

1. Universal Studios SG

South East Asia's premier theme park, USS is a great place to explore adventures and spend half a day

2. Fort Siloso

Pre-eminent historical place of World War II vintage

3. Tropical beaches

Siloso, Panjong and Palawan beaches at Sentosa offer fun and solitude equally, to the discerning traveller

4. Jewel Changi Airport

On the final day, reach Airport much in advance to discover the Jewel Changi attractions like the Rain Vortex, Forest Valley and Canopy Park, before flying back

ﭖﭖﭖ

Sentosa Boardwalk & Monorail (Top) and white sand
Sentosa beaches (bottom)

TWENTY

Jewel Changi: Rain Vortex, Forest Valley & Canopy Park, Changi Experience Studio and GST Refund Claim at Airport– Day 8

Day 8 at Singapore was a regular start as Yashika and Aditya decided to laze around the hotel's magnificent landscaped free-form pool, at the doorsteps of the beach villas that have a direct access. After about 45 minutes, they proceeded for the succinct western breakfast spread at the appointed hour. Post freshening up, it was time to say a fond goodbye to the warm caring Equarius staff. The Kumars left RWS Sentosa after a delightfully quick hotel check-out experience.

Taking their buggy shuttle to the waiting taxi by 11:30 AM, they reached Changi Airport via East coast parkway in about 25 minutes. Their return Air India flight was from passenger terminal building, PTB 1. They reached around noon for 7.45 PM flight, so as to have some time in hand for exploring Jewel Changi, which Jyoti had read rave reviews of.

The first pit stop at Changi airport was the eTRS self-help kiosks at terminal 1; where the Kumar's stopped by to scan their passports and apply for GST refund in cash/credit card under Tourist Refund Scheme (TRS) program. By applying at the eTRS kiosk in advance, the Kumar's would know if they had to budget more time for showing purchases to Customs for inspection or if they could directly proceed to Central Refund counter after Departure immigration with passport to collect the cash refund – they were happy to learn it was the latter option.

The family then proceeded to Jewel Changi, which's connected to the arrival hall of terminal 1, level 1 and was a short walk away. While certain airlines provide early check-in facility at level 1 of Jewel Changi, the Kumars kept the heavy luggage at the baggage storage counter at nominal fee and then proceeded to grab a bite. If the airline offers early check-in facility additionally from Jewel Changi, one could apply for refund at the GST counters at Jewel level1 and check-in luggage directly without paying any additional baggage storage fee.

Jewel Changi, located between terminals T2 &T3, is a huge complex spanning 10 storeys – five above-ground and five basement levels. It includes gardens, attractions, a hotel, about 300 retail and multitude of dining outlets. Enthusiasts can also pilot a runway race, a simulated flight or play games inspired by airport check-in processes at the Changi Experience Studio on level 4.

Jyoti, Aditya & Yashika proceeded to check out the attractions at Jewel, both free and paid facilities. The Forest valley was most impressive with Sense art installations adding to the green experience. The tallest indoor waterfall, the rain vortex made for a great sight too. Both these attractions were dazzling and available at no additional fee to visitors. The highlight of the Jewel visit was the gigantic 14000sq metre Indoor wonderland- canopy park, that had a small entry charge but was well worth it.

It was time for some more snacking as all the sight-seeing at Jewel had made them tired and hungry. They gorged on burgers and fries at one of the many fast-food cafes before collecting their baggage and proceeding back to their flight terminal.

Reaching check-in counters well before time, the security check and departure immigration was a smooth affair. While the girls were window shopping at the Changi duty free having spent most of their monies, it was time for Aditya to collect the GST refund from the central refund counter. Jyoti was in for a surprise as she couldn't believe that all their previous shopping had yielded a cool SGD 95 refund.

Acting like a teenager who's just been gifted some pocket money, Jyoti spent most of it on the imitation jewellery bargains and cosmetics at the duty-free, which she got packed in sealed bags lest they create a problem while boarding. She didn't buy any large bottles as Yashika reminded her that any liquids, aerosols or gels in containers larger than 100ml had to be kept in check-in luggage. And the remainder money was earmarked for checking out gifting goodies post arrival at Mumbai duty free.

The Kumars cheerfully boarded the return flight at Changi with fond memories of a delightful Singapore holiday experience.

❦❦❦

Equarius Hotel landscaped pool with cablecar sky view,
courtesy Resorts World Sentosa (Top) and Rain Vortex,
Forest Canopy & Skytrain at Jewel Changi Airport (bottom)

ᐁᐁᐁ

Thank You

ᐁᐁᐁ

www.ingramcontent.com/pod-product-compliance
Lightning Source LLC
Chambersburg PA
CBHW031319130726
47988CB00007B/2896